Seeds of Thought

Lamar McDougald

Life Chronicles Publishing
Give your life a voice!

ISBN-10: 099891147X

ISBN-13: 978-0998911472

Cover Design: Tatyana Collette

Life Chronicles Publishing

lifechroniclespublishing.com

Creative Editor: Sharon Blake

Dedication

To: Love, humanity, and the inner child within us all.

Contents

Prologue

This book is a guide to help those who feel like they are searching for something become aware that they are the missing puzzle piece they seek. Instinctively we look to fill these voids outside of ourselves; this leads us to feel like we are at the same old crossroads of search and discovery. The mission of this book is to help direct people back to love, restore complete mental freedom, and re-kindle the creative & artistic minds we all have.

This book is designed to be a creative artistic piece of literature.

JANUARY

Jan 1st

Self-love

Write 8 things that you LOVE about yourself. Get creative, it can be anything.

Jan 2nd Rule of thumb

Instead of judging people, just view everyone like a child that's bringing home an art drawing for you. It's not to be judged, or critiqued, but to be enjoyed and appreciated for what it is.

Jan 3rd

Trust your heart.

Jan 4th Perspective

Imagine if you approached everyday with the mentality of; I'm about to clock in for a 24-hour work shift of getting to know me. Only taking a break when you're sleeping. Make getting to know you a daily job. 24 hours a day. 7 days a week.

Jan 5th

Continue to work on mastering the art of discipline daily: Remember if you aren't disciplined...how can you judge others when they display a lack of it?

Jan 6th — Ask Yourself

Would your 10-year-old self be happy with who you've become and where you are in life?

Jan 7th

Spend 30 seconds 5x's today alone, just focusing on breathing. (inhaling and exhaling)

Jan 8th

Let all that you do be out of love. If you're doing something you don't love... why do you allow yourself to continue to do it?

Jan 9th

Let go of who you have become. Let go of what was created and molded by fear. To become who you truly are and that's just love. Love in human form.

Jan 10th Center

Take 10 deep breaths right now as big, slow, and controlled as you can. With every exhale experience allow the feeling of weight to be removed off your shoulders. Notice how you feel now, oppose to before doing it. I challenge you to take ten, 10 second interval deep breath moments throughout your day.

Jan11th Give love

Today give a hug to someone to you don't know.

Jan 12th Reconnect

Spend at least 10 minutes in nature today. Walking around on the ground without shoes. Allow mother earth to recharge you and reground you.

Jan 13th

That something that you are looking for is thyself. No longer search for it. Home is where that is. Your heart is home. You are love. So, you are what you're seeking. And until you find yourself, (love) you will continue to feel as if something is missing. Come home.

Jan 14th Monthly drawing

Think back to your childhood and visualize something from that time. Capture that image. Now draw it. No expectations. No worrying about if you're doing it right or how it looks. Just being free and allowing creativity to take over.

Jan 15th Time for a break

I challenge you to spend the first and last 2 hours of your day for the next week off social media.

Jan 16th

Don't allow anything outside of yourself (people, places, and things) determine whether your day is going to be beautiful or not. You are in control. Now make every day the best one of your life.

Jan 17th

Meditation growth

Spend the first and last moments of your day breathing and focusing on inhaling and exhaling. Count down from 10 with your eyes closed. For about 5 minutes.

* If you find yourself losing focus just gently guide your mind back to counting down and breathing.

* Cultivate the present moment. Allow your breathing to be that focal point.

Jan 18th Give love

Today text your best friend and let them know how much you love and appreciate them for who they are. Tell them a few things you feel they are great at.

Jan 19th

Your life and energy/time should revolve around you. Not $$. Because one will give you internal fulfillment and love, and another will only give you temporary emotional fulfillment, (monetary happiness).

Jan 20th

Have you put some time and energy towards yourself today? (love and passion)

Jan 21st

Emotions come and go. All the emotions we face. We choose to experience and live through emotions like, happiness, sadness, feeling alone, and anger. All of these we can garner and obtain instantly. Which is why so many of us are addicted to things that bring us that instant happiness (money, food, sex).

Jan 22nd

These are state of being. Peace of mind, wholeness, centeredness, and balance. Which are developed overtime through DAILY Self-love, Self-awareness, and Self-discipline. It's not a quick instant fix of happy emotion. Like all the externals of life are. (food, money, sex)

Jan 23rd

Let go of the addiction of using externals to fix something that's internal. It's like trying to fit a rectangle inside a circle.

Jan 24th

Embrace the beautiful journey of self-realization. The only thing in life that's NEVER CHANGING and CONSTANT. Is change itself. Embrace growth. Get to know you.

Jan 25th

Take notes

Trees, plants, and nature., never stop growing. Regardless of how things around them evolve and change. Even when we cut them down, they always grow back. Even when we try to place cement over them. They will grow around it, through it, or on it. They will not allow anything to stop them from growing, evolving, and loving. We are all one in the same. Us and nature.

Jan 26th

Don't put a limit on how much love you have to offer, or who that love is exclusively for. Give love to everyone you encounter. Regardless if they have anything to offer you. Love freely and without expectations and always see yourself in others. So, by loving them, you're loving yourself.

Jan 27th

We are all soul brothers and sisters once you can begin to view everyone around you as your family. Make a point to see yourself in everyone. Your heart and ability to love grows. Because you begin to only see the love and positive in everyone, but you must first see this love in yourself.

Jan 28th

It will always and forever only be about love. Your higher self-will constantly remind you of this your whole life. Until you get with the program. Your heart is telling you what you NEED. Your ego is telling you what you want, but DO NOT NEED. It works nonstop to convinces you that you need it. Listen to your heart.

Jan 29th

Instead of approaching relationships only focused on what someone can offer/provide for you externally, especially intimate and personal relationships. Shift the focus to what a relationship can offer/provide you internally through love, care, support, and inspiration. Everything else follows.

Jan 30th Letting go of attachment

I challenge you today to spend 4-5 hours with your phone off, or without touching or using your phone. Our phone is just a tool. To be used when needed, not relied on heavily or attached to.

Jan 31st Ask yourself

Do you love yourself in the ways that you expect others to love you? Be honest.

FEBRUARY

(JUST BE AND ALLOW MONTH)

Just be and allow love to take over your pen and write 8 new things that you LOVE about yourself. Get creative, it can be anything.

Feb 2nd

Just be and allow love to free you from your ego.

Feb 3rd

Just be and allow love to free you from your need to control.

Feb 4th

Just be and allow love to take control of your life.

Feb 5th

Just be and allow love to bridge the gap between who you've become and who you are at the heart.

Feb 6th

Just be and allow love to usher you back into your authenticity.

Feb 7th

Just be and allow love to fuel your passions and creativity. You are artist. We're all artists.

Feb 8th

Just be and allow love to guide you, not fear

Feb 9th

Just be and allow love to reveal your worth to yourself.

Feb 10th

Just be and allow love to reconcile you with your inner childhood essence. The free you. The fearless you. The imaginative you. The full of love you.

Feb 11th

Just be and allow love to drive out the fear of change and uncertainty.

Feb 12th

Just be and allow love to harmonize differences.

Feb 13th

Just be and allow love to give you the courage to remove yourself, any situation, and circumstances that are draining your energy. Emotionally, spiritually, physically, and mentally.

Feb 14th

Just be and allow love to free you from your judgmental nature.

Feb 15th

Just be and allow love to strip away the false identity and image of self you've created and associated with that is not yourself.

Feb 16th

Just be and allow love to free you from toxic thinking. Meditate.

Feb 17th

Just be and allow love to free you from the negative connotations you've created about yourself.

Feb 18th

Just be and allow love to break down the walls that have had you barricaded from your heart space and authenticity.

Feb 19th

Just be and allow love to produce more love.

Feb 20th

Just be and allow love to break what you may feel is an inability to be vulnerable.

Feb 21st

Just be and allow love to give you the strength to face all the toxic thoughts that you ignore daily. So that you can face them and let them go. So that they no longer have a hold and control over you.

Feb 22nd

Just be and allow love to free your mind.

Feb 23rd

Just be and allow love to remove you from anything that can cause separation from love. (religion, nationality, skin color) (beliefs)

Feb 24th

Just be and allow love to transform what may have been initially perceived as heart ache to something that produces more self-love.

Feb 25th

Just be and allow love to aid you in your imagination and creative mind.

Feb 26th

Just be and allow love (your heart) to make the decisions for you.

Feb 27th

Just be and allow love to be your only BELIEF.

Feb 28th

Just be and allow love to be your mirror.

MARCH

Mar 1st

Self-love

Write 8 things that you LOVE about yourself. Get creative it can be anything.

Mar 2nd

Remember love will never be apart from you. So never let any situation or circumstance affect your ability to give and receive love fully.

Mar 3rd

Spend 30 seconds 5 different x's alone today just focusing on inhaling and exhaling (breathing).

Mar 4th Repeat

Love flows through me. Love flows to me. Love flows around me.

Mar 5th

In all situations with people, places, and things. Before acting on them and saying or doing anything you may or may not regret. Do not accept. Do not reject. But contemplate all aspects of the situation. Breathe. Then make your decision and act accordingly. Always acting out of love.

Mar 6th Repeat

I'm the author, creator, and architect of my life. I'm in control.

Mar 7th

If you consider each moment of your life to be beautiful and special. You owe it to yourself to be fully present and aware in each of those.

Mar 8th

Think about how many things you don't do. Because you are in fear of what others will think, (family, friends, partner and society). Now think about how many things you do, actually do, but are afraid to let people know because of the fear of what they will think. Let go of fear. Don't be afraid to be u.

Mar 9th Challenge

Today give out 10 compliments to people you don't know. Give love.

Mar 10th Listen to your heart

Our hearts are that little voice we hear that's saying, "you can do it". Listen to the voice that's saying "you shouldn't say that" before you say something hurtful to someone. But we have the volume so low on our hearts that we can never hear it, or we ignore it. Turn down the volume in your mind that's playing the songs of fear, hate, insecurities, doubt.

Mar 11th Focus on the good

Stop allowing news and media outlets to drain you of your energy. Creating this narrative that things are just all bad. When that is not always the case. People are becoming more connected. Love is circulating.

Mar 12th Reconnect

Spend at least 10 minutes in nature today. Walking the ground without shoes. Allow mother earth to recharge and reground you.

March 13th

Love is the only truth. If you believe that, you know that love does not hurt, it does not contain fear, separate people, and create wars. But guess what does? Religion, nationality, backgrounds, political views, and skin color. (beliefs) Let go of these beliefs that separate not only yourself but humanity from love.

Mar 14th

Don't allow the god concept to put you in fear. God is love. You are love. You are god. All living beings are all connected. (earth, humans, nature, animals) (love) We are all love. So now, let's go back home to love.

Mar 15th

Perspective

Love is belief. You are love. So, with belief. (love thyself) You can do anything.

Mar 16th Meditation growth

Spend the first and last moments of your day breathing and focusing on you. Inhale and exhale while counting down from 10 with your eyes closed. For about 5 minutes.

* If you find yourself losing focus just gently guide your mind back to counting and breathing.

* Cultivate the moment and breathe.

Mar 17th Monthly drawing

Think back to childhood and visualize something from that time. Capture that image. Now draw it. No expectations. No worrying about if you're doing it right or how it looks. Just be free and allow creativity to take over.

Mar 18th

Love is the key: Love, love.

Mar 19th

Life and the World is your canvas. Are you going to be the one that's holding the paint brush? Or are you going to allow self-doubt, insecurities, negative thoughts, fear of change and uncertainty to paint your canvas for you. Are you going to take back control of your life? Grab the paint brush and begin to paint the canvas the way you desire. Creating a life that is a beautiful work of art that you are proud of.

Mar 20th Focus on the good

Something can always be learned from any person, place, or thing. It's all about our perspective, and the beliefs that we draw out of experiences. Allow all that you take from an experience to be of positivity and love. So that it can help you learn and grow closer to yourself.

Mar 21st

No longer be a slave to your thoughts but become a witness to them. Sit back and observe them. Don't just dive into each and every thought that comes across your mind. Just spend time observing them so that it's easier to recognize which thoughts are coming from your heart and which ones are from ego. Become the witness.

Mar 22nd

My open book journal: To Anita,

Someone I've admired from a far.

Someone I aspire to be more like.

Someone I've sat and listen to stories about with excitement in my mind and joy in my heart. As if I was a kid listening to tales of my favorite superhero.

Someone who makes me have a deeper appreciation for nature, plants, and herbs.

Someone that has the qualities and values I would hope my daughter and future wife embodies.

Someone who has a heart perfectly crafted to love and nurture.

Someone everyone could learn a great deal from.

Someone deserving of an insurmountable amount of love.

That someone... Is you.

With love.

Mar 23rd

Liberate yourself from anything you felt you've done wrong against someone so that it no longer has a hold on you internally and emotionally. Sometimes you must endure through situations that appear to be uncomfortable to grow and meet love on the other side.

Mar 24th

Remember you come first. YOU (your heart). All other titles (job, husband, wife, etc.) that you may carry always should come second. Are YOU happy? If you always make sure that you are full and complete within your heart. Those other titles become easier to maintain.

Mar 25th Rule of thumb

When it comes to creativity always be real 1st, and then from there have fun being creative without limits. Remember every piece of art you create is UNIQUE and BEAUTIFUL because YOU created. There is only ONE YOU. So, everything you do is 1 of 1. It's not to be judged or compared to others but appreciated and enjoyed because you created it.

Mar 26th Perspective

Love will always exist. We are love in human flesh. All living beings are love. Earth is love. Nature is love. With this said, we must stop hurting, killing, and undervaluing the love around us. Stop destroying love. And let's appreciate it and build up the love inside of us as well as around us.

Mar 27th Just breathe

I challenge you to belly breathe right now, and 5 times throughout the day. Placing your hands on your belly and experiencing the rise and fall of your belly. With each inhale and exhale. Always taking note of how you feel before and after.

Mar 28th Letting go of attachment

I challenge you today to spend 3-5 hours with your phone off, or without touching or using your phone. Our phone is just a tool. To be used when needed, not relied on heavily or attached to.

Mar 29th Ask yourself

What does Love mean to you?

Mar 30th Ask yourself

Do you remember the first time you fell in love and what that felt like? Positive reminiscing.

APRIL

Apr 1st Self-love

Write 8 things that you LOVE about yourself. Get creative it can be anything.

Apr 2nd Perspective:

Nothing specifically happens for a reason. We define the meaning of our experiences. Let what you choose to define your experiences, be that of love or positivity.

Apr 3rd Notes to self

Authenticity is one of the most beautiful qualities someone can have. So, embrace being you. Let the best part about you, be you being you.

Apr 4th Notes to self

Less is always more, and knowledge is a waste of your idea space.

Apr 5th Perspective

Make it a point to see the beauty and love in all things throughout your day today, and then reflect on how your day was before bed. Notice how you are trying to change how you perceive things out of love. Birth more love for yourself. The more love you can recognize outside of yourself. The more love you can recognize within yourself.

Apr 6th

Spend 30 seconds 5 x's alone today just focusing on your inhale and exhale breathing.

April 7th

Daily to do list

See with love. Speak out of love. Hear out of love.

Apr 8th Ask yourself

Are you working your current job because you love it? Or does it stem from some type of fear? Is it fear of not being able to provide for yourself and or family?

Apr 9th Loving freely

Today give out 10 compliments to people you don't know. Give love just to get love.

Apr 10th Focus on the good

Always stay optimistic in everything you do. (self-love)

Apr 11th

Love is the only thing that exist (earth, nature, humans, animals). Which is us. Everything else is not real love (religion, nationality, languages). We are all love. We are all one. Love is the only thing that is so.

Apr 12th

Only love for thyself can drive out fear. Because thyself is love and love is the most powerful force in this life.

Apr 13th

Monthly drawing

Think back to your childhood and visualize something from that time. Capture that image. Now draw it. No expectations. No worrying about if you're doing it right or how it looks. Just being free and allowing creativity to take over.

Apr 14th

Are you making the decisions in your life or are your beliefs (fear, anxiety, fear of uncertainty, anger, fear of change, etc.) making the decisions for you?

Apr 15th — Meditation growth

Spend the first and last moments of your day breathing focusing on only inhaling, exhaling and counting down from 10 with your eyes closed. For about 5 minutes.

If you find yourself losing focus just gently guide your mind back to counting down and breathing.

* Cultivating the moment and breathing.

Apr 16th Perspective

All our experiences are meaningless. We define meaning in our experiences. So, always draw out the positivity and love in all your experiences. Focus on the good. Be aware of how what could be viewed as bad WOULD have affected you if you would have acted on the negative.

Apr 17th Give love

Today text or call 5 people you haven't talked to in a while. And just give them some type of loving and uplifting message.

Apr 18th Perspective

We are all love. Love is all we need. Once you allow love to be all you have; you become all that you need. And that is love. Whole. Fulfilled. Complete.

Apr 19th Daily to do list

Wake up as a caterpillar and be that beautiful butterfly by the end of the day. Treat each day as a new opportunity to: 1. Learn something new about yourself. 2. To grow closer to yourself (self-love) 3. To express yourself in some creative way. And 4. Of course, to give love.

Apr 20th Reevaluate

Always go back and revisit past relationships with friends, family and partners that may not have worked or where you didn't like the outcome. Instead of going back and focusing on what you feel the other person did or did not do. Focus on seeing how you could have given more love and been more open and understanding in the relationship and how things could have been and turned out a-lot different. Humble yourself. Open your heart. Grow more empathy.

Apr 21st Just breathe

I challenge you to belly breathe right now, and 5 times throughout the day. Placing your hands on your belly and experiencing the rise and fall of your belly. With each inhale and exhale. Always taking note of how you feel before and after.

Apr 22nd Ask yourself

Have you ever in your life fully committed to you? Has all your time, energy, and love gone towards figuring out you? Loving you? It's okay to be selfish sometimes with your energy and love so that you can grow and evolve into your best self.

April 23rd Letting go of old habits

Write down 3 bad habits that you feel has hindered your growth. Write down 3 reasons why you find it hard to let go of them. And write down 3 new habits you would like to create to replace the old bad ones.

April 24th

Ask yourself

What are some things that are really important to you that others tend to overlook?

April 25th

Accept who you are and love who are. If you don't, know who you are, how can you get mad when someone else doesn't.

April 26th Daily to-do list

CREATE MORE. CONSUME LESS. We were born creators, not a consumer. We are conditioned and made into consumers when we are constant creators. Express. Create.

April 27th Take notes

Even when attempted to be confined by man, nature always finds it way.

April 28th Take notes

Never allow yourself to be confined.

Even through what seems to be a permanent, and an unbreakable barrier.

Do not allow any force to stop its ability to grow and get where it needs to be.

This picture symbolizes many things.

But for me, it represents resilience.

The little clues from the universe and nature are all around us. We just need to be aware to recognize them.

April 29th Perspective

We all have that burning desire inside to create and express ourselves. Because we are all artists. So, approach every situation and circumstance as a blank canvas that you have the opportunity to leave a loving mark on. Grab your paint brush artist.

Apr 30th Ask yourself

Are you hard to love?

MAY

May 1st Self-love

Write 8 things that you LOVE about yourself. Get creative it can be anything.

May 2nd

Love is the key

Love is freeing and liberating.

May 3rd

Daily to-do list

Let everything you do be done out of love. Not fear.

May 4th

Notes to self

Everything I need is within me internally. So, anything externally is like added flavors on top. Good, but not needed.

May 5th

Stop approaching different situations, circumstances and people with the same approach expecting different results. Whatever you put in is what you get out. Let love be what you put in and see what comes out of it

May 6th

Why do you place expectations on people, situations, and circumstances continuously? To only be let down. Expect nothing but appreciate everything.

May 7th Perspective

Approach people, situations, and circumstances with a sense of curiosity, openness, and love. Instead of premeditated expectations and you will find yourself not being let down so often.

May 8th | Love is the key

Master the art of letting people just be.

May 9th | Monthly reconnect

If weather permits, spend 10 minutes outside, no shoes. Reconnecting with nature and earth. Because this place is our home and what we are made of, the earth is as well. So, the more we take care of it, essentially it is us taking better care of ourselves. Remember we are all connected. One love.

May 10th Daily to-do list

Make it a point daily to do some type of creating. Whether that is doodling, singing, or dancing. Whatever the form of creative expression, make sure you spend an adequate amount of time daily doing something. Create just as much as you consume externally.

May 11th Ask yourself

Am I a bigger fan of my favorite entertainer, actor, or athlete than I am myself? Is it easier for me to find nice things to say about them than it is for me to say about myself?

* Do you think they are unbelievable at what they do?

* Write down some things you think they are awesome at?

____

____

May 12th — Love is the key

Stop allowing something you cannot physically touch or see rule your life. Fear does not exist. We feel it and shape our lives around it. Let it go and take control of your life. Shape your life around love.

May 13th — Center

Take ten deep breaths right now as big, slow, and controlled as you can. With every exhale, experience the feeling of weight being removed from your shoulders. Notice how you feel now, as opposed to before you did it. I challenge you to take ten more 10-second interval deep breath moments throughout your day.

May 14th

Let go of who you think you are and how you're supposed to be or act. And just be.

May 15th

Spend 30 seconds 5 x's alone today just focusing on your inhale and exhale breathing.

May 16th Challenge

Today give a hug to someone you don't know. Give love.

May 17th Ask yourself

Does your first response to seeing or receiving positive, loving, and uplifting information create negative thoughts or annoyance? Ask yourself why it is you've become so separated from who you are at the core. (love)

May 18th Monthly drawing

Think back to your childhood and visualize something from that time. Capture that image. Now draw it. No expectations. No worrying about if you're doing it right or how it looks. Just being free and allowing creativity to take over.

May 19th Time for a break

I challenge you to spend the first and last 2 hours of your day for the next week off social media.

May 20th Love is the key

Love and love cannot be separated.

May 21st

From Lauryn Hill interlude 5: “The real you is more interesting than the fake somebody else.” Happy birthday to one of the greatest and influential artists there is.

May 22nd

I challenge you today to write down 3 things that you love doing. Things that give you the most internal fulfillment, (love) that only you can give you. Some form of self-expression (art). Ok, now after you write down those 3 things. Ask yourself how much energy have you been putting towards these?

May 23rd Ask yourself

Is the majority of my days spent doing exactly what I love? If not, when did this become my reality?

May 24th Ask yourself

When did I become afraid of love? Love being thyself. When did I begin to develop marginalized thinking? When did I lose my ability to be creative and imaginative? (childhood like essence) Have a conversation with yourself today, get to know you.

May 25th — Artist rule of thumb

Everything we do is an expression (art), and individually all of our forms of expression is perfect because it's OURS. It's not to be held to some standard. It's art. Instead of judging and comparing our expression (art) amongst each other. Let's just enjoy and embrace each other's art for what it is.

May 26th — Letting go of attachment

I challenge you today to spend 4-5 hours with your phone off, or without touching or using your phone. Our phone is just a tool. To be used when needed, not relied on heavily or attached to.

May 27th Love is the key

Allow love to be the only thing you're attached to and addicted to. Allow love to be your gateway drug. Love is the only healthy addiction.

May 28th Love is the key

Loving yourself fully makes it easier to love others around you freely without expecting them to fill YOUR half-empty cup. Allow self-love to fill that half-empty cup full.

May 29th Letting go of old habits part 2:

Write down 3 more bad habits that you feel has been hindering your growth. Write down 3 reasons why you find it hard to let go of them. Write down 3 new habits you would like to create to replace the old bad ones.

May 30th Ask yourself

What's something that you really appreciate about life and yourself at the current moment?

JUNE

June 1st Self-love

Write 8 things that you love about yourself. Get creative it can be anything.

June 2nd

You are the author of this story you call your life. If your life was a book, would it be a story you would enjoy reading? If not, only you can re-write it.

June 3rd

Do you know why it's so easy for us to point out the flaws, inconstancies, and transgressions of others? Because we ourselves are dealing with those very same things also. So, it's easy to point out those things when we see them in others as well. Let go of judging others. Allow others to serve as a mirror to you to show you what areas, you can grow in.

June 4th Perspective

If you're involved in a situation that you feel may be unfavorable for you. Simply add love and a positive perspective on the situation and watch how fast it begins to transform for you.

Jun3 5th Daily to do list

Replace "I can't" with "I'm able". Replace "I want" with "I have".

June 6th — Letting go of old habits

Release any habitual negative thought patterns you have about yourself, that has a hold on you. Allow them to fall away and be replaced by love and positive affirmations about yourself.

June 7th — Daily to do list

Tell yourself right now that you deserve whatever it is that you desire. No matter how unattainable you've made it seem. Tell yourself: You can. You are. You will obtain it.

June 8th Perspective

Remember you are what you attract. So whatever energy you're exuding and putting out there. It will always boomerang back to you.

June 9th Perspective

Everyone deserves to know what it feels like to be in love and that feeling to be truly mutual. If you're having doubts about mutual love, you too deserve it. If you have it. Cherish it. Nurture it. Appreciate it.

June 10th

Let the love you give yourself set the standard for others. BUT, understand the amount of love you give yourself could never be matched by anything or anyone. SO, you should never find yourself attached to any type of love externally. Expecting it to be able to compete with that love that you have for yourself.

June 11th

Spend 30 seconds 5 x's alone today just focusing on your inhale and exhale breathing.

June 12th Perspective

Let go of left brain thinking. It's marginalizing. 1+1 does not always equal 2. When two people procreate, most times it only results in 1 or more children. Reconnect with your right brain. The creative, imaginative, loving, free side. (childhood like essence)

June 13th Letting go of old habits

How could you ever judge someone for anything they have: 1. Said 2. Done 3. Thought. When at some point in your life you have: 1. Said 2. Done 3. Thought something that was not you. Let go of judging your brothers and sisters. Only see love.

June 14th Reconnect

Spend at least 10 minutes in nature today. Walking the ground without shoes. Allow mother earth to recharge and reground you.

June 15th Monthly drawing

Rethink to your childhood and visualize something from that time. Capture that image. Now draw it. No expectations. No worrying about if you're doing it right or how it looks. Just being free and allowing creativity to take over.

June 16th Reminder

2Pac cares if nobody else does. Happy Birthday to a legend, visionary, and one of my inspirations!

June 17th Monthly reconnect

If weather permits, spend just 10 minutes outside, no shoes. Reconnecting to nature and earth. Because this place is our home and what we are made of, earth is as well. So, the more we take care of it, it is essentially us taking better care of ourselves. Remember we are all connected. One love.

June 18th Letting go of old habits

No longer find comfort and reside in the feeling of pain and suffering. No longer settle for being undervalued and unappreciated.

June 19th Reevaluate

It's not about ignoring and masking the parts of you that you don't like or that you may be insecure about. But, bring them to your awareness to figuring out why you feel the way you do about yourself. Where do your insecurities come from? Turn what was once insecurities into confidence.

June 20th Love is the key

Life becomes a-lot easier once you realize you don't have to do this alone. We all are in this together. The me vs the world mentality develops when we're in a place of fear, not love. Survival of the fittest mentality has conditioned our minds. Collectively we should let this go and come closer together, opposed to further apart.

June 21st Love is the key

See yourself as love. See others as love. See nature as love. See all living beings as love. See earth as love. Once you can only see, feel, and hear love; you become just that, LOVE.

June 22nd

Question: How would u describe the feeling you experience when you're giving or receiving genuine love in one word?

June 23rd Letting go of old habits

Write down more 3 bad habits that you feel has been hindering your growth. Write down 3 reasons why you find it hard to let go of them. Write down 3 new habits you would like to create to replace the old bad ones.

June 24th

My open book journal: Written June 24th, 2017

What I've learned over this past year has been nothing short of beautiful. Learning that life isn't just happening, but reacting to our every thought, action, and perspective. Realizing once you allow life to just happen freely you begin to feel more comfortable in your being. Allowing love to guide you down your path. I've learned to accept myself for who I am, and not compare myself amongst others. Continuously providing myself with self-love, and the confidence that I've lacked my whole life. Understanding that I'm not here to be perfect, but to be authentic. Re-uniting myself with the one thing I've longed for, admired, and had the desire to feel and that is love. Love was never apart from me, but because of the situations and circumstances I found myself in what appeared to be anything but loving, I felt I was undeserving and not capable of receiving or giving love. I've learned to see love not only in myself, but in all situations, people, and circumstances. Also, that we all deserve to love, and be loved. Love will never be a part of us because it is who we are in our purest form, but we choose not to recognize that. We allow our ego, and experiences to mold us, instead of love. In a nutshell, I've learned to let love take back control of my life. And I'm beginning to find self-liberation and solidarity in my writing. So, this is me offering my vulnerable, raw, and unapologetic self to you.

With love.

June 25th — Visualization

Describe what you would consider to be your dream day. What would the most PERFECT day be like? What would you do? With who, what, when, where, and why? Get creative as possible.

June 26th

My open book journal: Written June 26th, 2017

I am no longer afraid to cry. I am no longer afraid to confront my emotions, and what I'm feeling inside. I am no longer masking my pain, confusion, and suffering from false happiness. I am no longer carrying emotional debts. I am no longer allowing love to be suppressed in my healing. I am allowing love to enter in and liberate me from my suffering and confusion I've carried. I am learning how to articulate and express what I'm experiencing internally, and emotionally into my words. I am no longer broken. I am no longer confused. I am no longer a slave to my suffering and pinned up aggression. I am no longer afraid to cry. I am free. I am whole. I am love.

June 27th Ask yourself

What's more important to you, money or peace of mind? Do your actions align with your answer. Care about your peace of mind and mental health the same as you do money and obtaining it.

June 28th Love is the key

Let go of worrying about what comes next. Focus on the present.

June 29th

Spend 5 minutes today just sitting outside. No cell phones. No technology. Just you and nature, rest and find peace in the quiet comfort of your mind. Re-connect with your surroundings. Re-center.

June 30th

Food for thought

The body is made of 70% water. The earth is made up of 70% water. We are born with everything we need. Us and nature, and earth are one in the same. Made up of all the same elements.

JULY

July 1st Self-love

Write 8 things that you LOVE about yourself. Get creative it can be anything.

July 2nd Daily to do list

Everyday love yourself in the way you'd love to be loved by another.

July 3rd Loving freely

Allow your love to shine in some way today.

July 4th Love is the key:

Trust in your heart. It is most trusted and reliable.

July 5th Reminder

You are able.

July 6th

My open book journal: Written July 6th, 2017

I'm thankful for everyone that has wronged me. Everyone that's taken advantage of my heart. Everyone that has undervalued me. Everyone that harmed me. Everyone that has not appreciated my love. Everyone that overlooked me. Everyone that has talked down on me. Everyone who has not taken the time to listen and understand me. Everyone that I've provided a shoulder to cry on, but when I needed a shoulder was nowhere to be found. Everyone who undervalued my love for them. I will forever be grateful for every single one of you. Because of you I no longer rely on outside love for my comfort. Because of you, I have a deeper appreciation for who I am, and myself. Because of you, I know my worth. Because of you, I've fallen in love with my love. Because of you, I've filled every void within myself that was once empty with my own love... Thank you, because of you I have reconciled with my love.

July 7th Daily to do list

Repeat these mantras: I accept. I accept who I am. I accept things I cannot change. I accept love. I accept uncertainty. I accept change.

July 8th

Today I challenge you to create as much as you consume: If you spend 4 hours watching tv spend 4 hours drawing or writing. If you spend 2+ hours on social media, spend 2+ hours outside in nature.

July 9th Challenge

Spend 30 seconds 5 x's alone today just focusing on your inhale and exhale breathing.

July 10th

Dear, mom.

The perfect imperfection of nature reminds me of you.

The beautiful harmony and soothing sound of the ocean and ocean waves reminds me of you.

The feeling of being at home reminds me of you.

The mesmerizing view of a graceful sunrise and sunset reminds me of you.

The love and laughter of a child reminds me of you.

All things that are love remind me of you.

That's because you are love.

I can only hear, see, and feel love.

Because myself and all living beings are.

Because we all came from LOVE.

Thank you.

Dedicated to my mother, and all mothers including mother nature and mother earth.

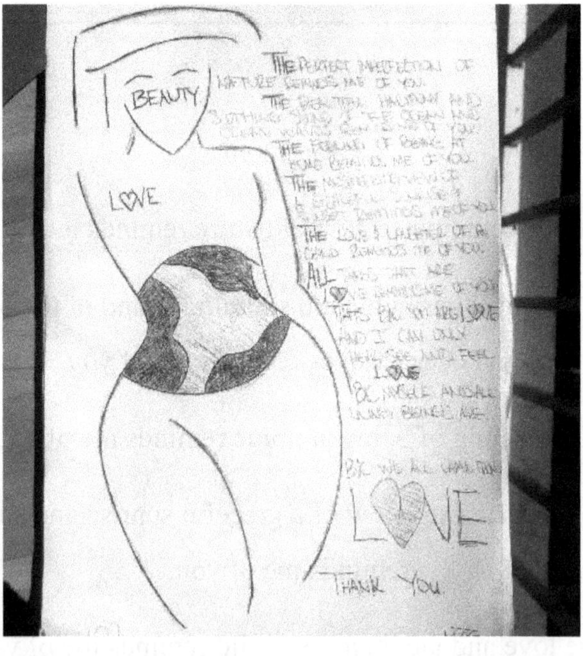

July 11th

Love is the key

No longer continue to keep the same mind frame and then wonder why you cannot conquer your minds fully. You must break yourself down completely to the core. Not one foot in and One foot out. If so, that's the results you will get.

July 12th

Challenge

Today give a hug to someone you don't know. Give love.

July 13th Reevaluate

Instead of ignoring those thoughts that you have buried deep within the confinement of your mind. Bring awareness to them. Recognize them. Relive them. Experience them again. See how they've molded you negatively and caused you to create self-inflicting thoughts and beliefs that you carry today.

July 14th Food for thought

We are all God and God is love. Reconnect with yourself and that is love. (god)

July 15th Center

Take ten deep breaths right now as big, slow, and controlled as you can. With every exhale, experience the feeling of weight being removed from your shoulders. Notice how you feel now, as opposed to before you did it. I challenge you to take ten more 10-second interval deep breath moments throughout your day.

July 16th Reevaluate

Do you have any unsettled resentment or hurtful thoughts, feelings, views, and emotions towards certain situations with your parents? From childhood until now. (we all may) Revisit these unloving thoughts and beliefs that have been created from these experiences. Investigate how they have affected you and molded you negatively. And how they have drawn you away from yourself (love), now let it go. Understand the internal battle you are facing daily. Your parents have faced them as well. Liberate yourself from these feelings. Forgive.

July 17th   Love is the key

In this life you only need love. But you already are love. You were born into this life having everything you need (thyself, which is love.) So, if you have that feeling as if you “need” something. Then love for thyself is missing.

July 18th   Love is the key

Passion is love for thyself. No longer, look for a specific thing as your passion. You are what you are seeking. Which is yourself. (love) Being you is that passion you desire, and you creatively expressing yourself. Just be.

July 19th

Love is the key

Fall back in love with yourself.

July 20th

Monthly drawing

Think back to your childhood and visualize something from that time. Capture that image. Now draw it. No expectations. No worrying about if you're doing it right or how it looks. Just be free and allow creativity to take over.

July 21st Just breathe

Any time you feel negative, fearful, or anything other than love coming across your mind or in your thought bubble, just breathe. Just breathe. Recognize it, don't ignore it. See where it came from, then let it go. Just breathe.

July 22nd Love is the key

You are already perfect. You were crafted perfectly. We are all perfect imperfections. We are all butterflies constantly going through the caterpillar to butterfly phase. Growth and change are a part of life. Embrace it. U already are what u desire, just allow yourself to be.

July 23rd Food for thought

Put the same effort and energy we use to obtain externals things to get to know yourself more. You'd have less externally, but more peace of mind and love.

July 24th Love is the key

Putting most of your time/energy into obtaining more should never be at the expense of sacrificing energy to getting to know you more. (love)

July 25th Love is the key

When you are on a self-growth journey you have to view yourself/heart as a house, and when you are doing a home makeover you can't just makeover the kitchen, and not the rest of the house. It must be a holistic growth journey. Every area of your life must undergo a makeover because everything is connected. The entire house must be worked on, not just the front yard and exterior of the house. Masking won't do. Clean the inside and out. Full holistic growth.

July 26th Love is the key

Love has the ability to drive out ANY and EVERYTHING we are battling internally in our minds. Stop avoiding the one thing that can fix everything. (love) All things externally will never fix the internal issues. It can temporarily fix it or assist us in ignoring it. But ignoring the issue is not fixing it. It's just masking it. Love is the only thing that can-heal and drive out all of the negative and conflicting thoughts and beliefs that may reside in our mind. Love is the key.

July 27th

Question: How would you describe love in one word?

July 28th

Question: What is love to you?

July 29th

Reevaluate

I'd like for you to go back and reevaluate the days of April 23rd, May 29th, June 23rd. Look at all the bad habits you wrote down and the reasons why you felt they were hard to let go of at the time. Examine the new thoughts you created to replace the bad habits. Ask yourself, have I implemented the new habits? Have I let go of the old? Do I still struggle with the reasons why I find it hard to let go of old habits?

July 30th

Visualization: Describe your ideal typical day to day life and what it would look like. What you would be doing, and how it would make you feel? Get creative.

AUGUST

Aug 1st Self-love

Write 8 things that you LOVE about yourself. Get creative it can be anything.

Aug 2nd

You are able to accomplish and manifest whatever it is that you desire in this life. Repeat this to yourself whenever a self-doubting thought arises in your mind today.

Aug 3rd — Love is the key

Love is the greatest remedy. Apply love to any situation and it will heal it.

Aug 4th Love is the key

Only view yourself as love.

Aug 5th Remember

To liberate yourself from negative thoughts and beliefs that have held you captive. Get back to the core of how these thoughts and beliefs developed. Recognize them. Live with them. Break them down to see how they molded you. Then, let them go. No longer give them authority and power, in your mind.

Aug 6th

Spend 30 seconds 5 x's alone today just focusing on your inhale and exhale breathing.

Aug 7th

Challenge

Today give a hug to someone you don't know. Give love.

Aug 8th Center

Spend ten minutes today resting in your breath and thoughts. No expectations. Just with a sense of curiosity and openness. Don't be afraid of what thoughts cross your mind.

Aug 9th Food for thought

The solution is simple for humanity. What's stopping people from coming together? Religion, nationality, skin color, languages, and beliefs. We have identified the problem. So logically thinking it would make sense to get rid of that which is causing the problem to reach what we are seeking. Truth. (love) (thyself)

Aug 10th Monthly drawing

Think back to your childhood and visualize something from that time. Capture that image. Now draw it. No expectations. No worrying about if you're doing it right or how it looks. Just being free and allowing creativity to take over.

Aug 11th Love is the key

You are your most valuable asset. You are love. Love is art. Now invest in you.

Aug 12th — Time for a break

I challenge you to spend the first and last 2-hours of your day for the next week off social media.

Aug 13th — Love is the key

Once you apply more love to yourself. Everything else around you then appears, feels, and becomes more loving.

Aug 14th Perspective

Individually we are all running our own race, as an individual we are a part of. Therefore, you are running a one-man race that you already have won. So, let go of thinking you must live up to some standard or expectations. When you already are the standard. Perspective.

Aug 15th Letting go of old habits

Let go of competition amongst others. You have already won. Instead of wanting to beat our next man. Let's applaud him/her and encourage them on their individual race, that they've already won. We in this together. (unity)

Aug 16th Reminder

You are love and you are loved.

Aug 17th Reminder

Love, love.

Aug 18th Daily to do list

Learn to always respond to negativity with compassion and love.

Aug 19th Reminder

Everything outside of yourself is to be used as a tool to help you grow closer to yourself. Not to be attached to, abused, or reliant on. You have all the tools within you already to accomplish all that you need. Balance.

Aug 20th

We all are fighting the same internal battle. Do not let that external by product of the internal battle cause you to view and judge your brothers and sisters because of this external difference. Because all our problems are seemingly from the same place. Internally, our mind.

Aug 21st

Love is the key

Value the life of all beings. (mother earth, mother nature, animals, humans)

Aug 22nd Daily to do list

Listen twice as much as you speak. Any moment you take the time to thoroughly listen to other people's opinions and views it gives you more insight on them and how they view things. Which helps you grow closer to that person and understand them more. Opposed to always placing your opinions on others and thinking your views are the best way. Stay open. Stay humble.

Aug 23rd Daily to do list

Find liberation internally through your creativity. Allow personal gratification and emotional happiness to come from the inside, by you expressing and being creative. Let go of the reliance of instant gratification from people, place, and things outside of yourself. (FOOD, SEX, MONEY, MATERIAL THINGS)

Aug 24th Perspective

CHANGE. The one thing in life that is always occurring. Every second, minute, and day. We are always changing and evolving internally and externally (mind and body) so no longer be afraid of something that is a natural part of life. Embrace change and growth.

Aug 25th Give love

Today text or call 5 people you haven't talked to in a while. Send them some type of loving and uplifting message.

Aug 26th Food for thought

Kids are in a place of pure love. Most EVERYONE has a special place in their hearts for kids. Many teens and adults are no longer in a place of pure love, but more so, live in fear, self-hate, anger, confusion, jealously, and competition. We expect kids to learn from adults who are trying to regain what kids already have (pure love). Maybe we should be learning from kids, instead of trying to teach them.

Aug 27th Notes to self

Don't allow the fear of failure to stop you from exploring a venture you are curious about. You have that desire and curiosity to explore this because your higher self (heart) knows you will be able to accomplish whatever comes to you along your path.

Aug 28th Notes to self

Don't allow "what it's going to take" to accomplish or reach a goal overwhelm you mentally to where you lose interest in even accomplishing that goal. Remember to always embrace the journey. The destination is only the cherry on top.

Aug 29th Ask yourself

Ask yourself: If what you're doing isn't growing you closer to yourself. You, being love. Why are you doing it?!

Aug 30th Love is the key

The one thing that can help solve all our problems is the one thing that most of us are afraid of, avoiding, and running away from is love. To fully live through love U must know who you are. Because you are love. So, once you find yourself. You find love.

Aug 31st

JUST BE.

SEPTEMBER

Sept 1st Self-love

Write 8 things that you LOVE about yourself. Get creative it can be anything.

Sept 2nd Center

Take ten deep breaths right now as big, slow, and controlled as you can. With every exhale experience the feeling of weight being removed from your shoulders. Notice how you feel now, as opposed to before you did it. I challenge you to take ten more 10-second interval deep breath moments throughout your day.

Sept 3rd Love is the key

Love is seeing the beauty in all people, places, and things.

Sept 4th

JUST BE.

Sept 5th

Love is the key

Never find relief in suppressing emotions. Allow love to come in and clear out those emotional debts.

Sept 6th Daily to do list

Repeat these mantras: I create. I create art. I create love. I create opportunities for myself. I create space and stillness in my mind.

Sept 7th Ask yourself

Are you controlling your own time, or are you allowing time to control you?

Sept 8th Notes to self

Stop letting something you can't even touch, feel, or see (fear) stop you from doing what you desire.

Sept 9th Food for thought

How you allow people to treat you is a very good depiction of how you view and value yourself. SO, KNOW your worth. Value who you are and don't allow anyone to treat you in a way that does not align with that. More importantly actively practice self-love on a daily basis.

Sept 10th

Spend 30 seconds 5 x's alone today just focusing on your inhale and exhale breathing.

Sept 11th Daily to do list

Replace "I can't "with "I am able", replace "I want" with "I have."

Sept 12th Reminder

There is no such thing as a good or bad decision made. What we may consider as good and bad can be found in all decisions we've ever made in life. So, make all your decisions freely and with confidence. Don't over think. Don't analyze. Don't be afraid. Just do it. Have a clear intent and understand the universe has your back.

Sept 13th Letting go of old habits

Never sweep pain under the carpet learn how to face your emotions head on, so that they won't have a hold on you.

Sept 14th Perspective

Use every situation that may appear to be working against you to open up your heart even more.

Sept 15th Reminder

You are what you attract. So whatever energy you're exuding or putting out there will always boomerang back to you.

Sept 16th Ask yourself

Are you more focused on the "what if" aspect of a person, place, or thing? Opposed to just focusing on the good?

Sept 17th

My open book journal; Written June 14th, 2018

I have nothing but love for the mother of my child. I made mistakes when we were together and during the pregnancy. I'm not perfect, and I can admit my past transgressions. I was going through a rough stage in life while I was with her. I used her as a punching bag.... You never realize the hurt you caused a person until after the damage has been done. Because you're so lost, caught up, and stuck within the solidity of your mind. Like anyone else I did not know how to handle what I was dealing with emotionally at the time.

So, it was hard for me to receive and appreciate love when I had it. Because I did not have a love for myself at the time. I say that to say this. I'm not perfect. But that's the thing it's not about being perfect. It's about being authentic, and continually growing and figuring it out. Unfortunately, sometimes along that path we drag people along for our own personal selfish reasons. Fear of being lonely being is one example. So, if you find yourself in a situation that I was in. Being a part of a relationship, I wasn't ready for. Being with someone when I wasn't prepared to commit. Expecting someone to love parts of me I didn't love myself. Placing expectations on someone that I couldn't even fulfill for me. Dragging someone along my path of self-discovery at the expense of their feelings. Being selfish. Not ready to open up and staying closed off to someone that just wanted to love me. These are the things we do not even realize we are doing when we are Kicking dirt in the face of someone that just wants to love you. I can look back now and admit to these mistakes. And say, I was wrong. Yes, I have grown, evolved, and learned from mistakes tremendously. Unfortunately, it was at the expense of her feelings and others. So, I'm sharing this with you because I believe in love, it's all about experiences, learning and growing from them positively and allowing those experiences to open up your heart and mind more. But when you're not taught how to handle or approach it in that manner it could cause not only hurt and pain to yourself but someone else also. So yes, experiences are beautiful. But having the wisdom to not put yourself in situations that could harm others is more important. Know when you need to grow and figure things out for you. Before trying to bring another soul/heart into the picture. Don't be afraid of being alone. Don't fear love. Breaking yourself down and owning up to all the hurt you've caused others in the past is uncomfortable. But it's necessary to let go of that person you thought you were to become who you know you are. And being... Authentic. Forgiving of yourself. Having empathy for others. More importantly, allowing love to come in and do a home makeover internally is the key. So again, I've shared all of this with you. To show people that although I'm in this permanent place of love now. It didn't begin this way; It was a long journey. Filled with hurt, confusion, and pain that I placed on myself and others that could have been avoided. Maybe by me being vulnerable and sharing my story. It could help someone avoid what I had to go through to get here. Much love.

Sept 18th Self-love practice

Today go in your room and close the door and play your favorite song as loud as you can. Just dance as crazy and freeing, and as loose as you can. Be free. Don't worry about how you are looking. Be free. If you find this difficult and hard to do. Because of the judgements you have about yourself. Ask yourself why it is so hard for me to just be myself. Why can't I be myself when no one is looking? Who am I when everyone else is around?

Sept 19th Reconnect

Spend at least 10 minutes in (mother) nature today. Walking the ground without shoes. Allow mother earth to recharge and reground you.

Sept 20th Take notes

(Mother) nature never needs a filter or alterations. It is perfect in every way and neither do you. You were born perfect. Us and nature are one in the same. (love)

Sept 21th Food for thought

How can you say you represent something that's the truth? If what you promote looks down on, judges and or believes what you represent is better than another belief, religion or group of people. (separation) Love brings people together, it does not cause separation. Love is the only truth. Let's bridge this gap.

Sept 22nd Notes to self

You are the only one responsible for your own fulfillment, joy, and happiness. No one can love you the way you love you.

Sept 23rd Daily to do list

Take back control of your body. Eat what is in natural rhythm with (e(art)h) and your vehicle (flesh) which is made up of the same elements. If you can create discipline in your body. It makes it easier to do so in your mind.

Sept 24th Monthly drawing

Think back to your childhood and visualize something from that time. Capture that image. Now draw it. No expectations. No worrying about if you're doing it right or how it looks. Just being free and allowing creativity to take over.

Sept 25th Monthly reconnect

If weather permits, spend just 10 minutes outside, no shoes. Reconnecting to nature and earth. Because this place is our home and it is what we are made of, earth is as well. So, the more we take care of it, it is essentially us taken better care of ourselves. Remember we are all connected. One love.

Sept 26th Reminder

Expressing yourself becomes easier and easier. Once u realize u are art. Let go of other beliefs that are contradictions. There is only one real BELIEF, that is (love) love being (art) (earth, nature, all livings beings) embrace and love who you are. U are art. We're all artist.

Sept 27th Notes to self

You are enough. The you that cannot to be seen, touched, or grabbed. The you that only can be felt internally (love).

Sept 28th Notes to self

Remain balanced, fearless, and full of love internally regardless of the external changes and circumstances.

Sept 29th Love is the key

Love thyself. Love thy neighbor. Love all living beings (mother nature, mother earth, all livings beings) because we are one love.

Sept 30th Reminder

You are not within the confinement of your flesh (body), your body is within the confinement of your soul. Your soul is infinite and limitless.

OCTOBER

Oct 1st Self-love

Write 8 things that you LOVE about yourself. Get creative it can be anything.

Oct 2nd Love is the key

Develop internal love. Instead of seeking external love.

Oct 3rd Daily to do list

Let your tongue mirror your heart.

Oct 4th Love is the key

Love should always be the glue that holds a relationship together.

Oct 5th Love is the key

Allow love to be your only truth.

Oct 6th Love is the key

Allow love to be your compass.

Oct 7th Letting go of old habits

Let go of the habit of looking outside of yourself to fill voids that are within you. Only you can fill those internal voids with love.

Oct 8th — Focus on the good

We are constantly going through life living through experiences. Just be and allow those experiences to give birth to more love, self-awareness, wisdom, understanding and clarity. Instead of hurting, pain, regret, suffering and confusion.

Oct 9th — Love is the key

How can you expect someone to love parts of you that you don't love yourself? Replace those negative beliefs you have about yourself, with positive affirmations and love.

Oct 10th   Notes to self

Never let anyone treat or value you less. How much do you treat and value yourself?

2

Oct 11th

Repeat these mantras: I embrace. I embrace love. I embrace uncertainty and change. I embrace the journey not the destination. I embrace loved ones. I embrace my authenticity.

Oct 12th

Spend 30 seconds 5 x's alone today just focusing on your inhale and exhale breathing

---

Oct 13th

Love is the key

Release any habitual negative thought patterns you have about yourself that has a hold on you. Allow them to fall away and be replaced by love and positive affirmations about yourself.

Oct 14th

You must create that balance and harmony between your heart and mind or there will always be an inner conflict between the two. Because the heart always operates out of love. Opposed to the mind that could be led by the ego, fear, and or many different types of emotions.

Oct 15th

Love is the key

Follow your heart. It will guide you back home to love. Don't allow fear to be the wall standing in between you and love. Allow more love in to help tear down that wall.

Oct 16th

Love thyself. Reconnect with yourself. Don't allow any person place or thing to create a gap between you and yourself.

Oct 17th

Question: Why does love scare people? (fear) Why are you afraid of who you are? (love) When will stop being more interested in figuring out something that's negative than exploring something that's more loving?

Oct 18th Monthly drawing

Think back to your childhood and visualize something from your childhood. Capture that image. Now draw it. No expectations. No worrying about if you're doing it right or how it looks. Just being free and allowing creativity to take over.

Oct 19th Monthly reconnect

If weather permits, spend just 10 minutes outside, no shoes. Reconnecting to nature and earth. Because this place is our home and what we are made of, earth is as well. So, the more we take care of it, it is essentially us taken better care of ourselves. Remember we are all connected. One love.

Oct 20th Food for thought

The one thing we avoid most, is also the one thing that we desire most (love). Just love.

Oct 21st Reminder

You are love and you are loved.

Oct 22nd Perspective

You can be whoever you have a desire to be and do whatever you have a desire to do. Don't marginalize yourself into thinking you can only do 1 thing. U are infinite. Go be all you know you can be.

Oct 23rd Ask yourself

Do I want to look back on life full of regret? Or do I want to say, I did exactly what I wanted and loved?

Oct 24th

Why does so much envy and competition exist amongst friend groups or people we are close with? Instead of thinking we are in competition and having envious thoughts towards the people we say we love and are friends with let's just love them for who they are and cheer them on. Nothing less.

Oct 25th

Love is the key

The one thing that we avoid the most, is the solution to all our issues. (love)

Oct 26th

Marriage is the union of love and love. To be in a real marriage, you must be back in a place of pure love internally (childhood like essence). Before deciding to unify with another soul/partner understand that if you YOURSELF are not in a place of pure love and internal fulfillment; you will Instinctively place expectations on our partner for internal fulfillment. When it's a task only you can accomplish.

Oct 27th Love is the key

Only love can draw you closer to love.

Oct 28th

Daily self-love is the key to letting go of the person you have become. You have been created and molded by all the different experiences you have been through in life and the negative beliefs and thoughts you have learned from said experiences.

Oct 29th

Love is the key

Self-love reconnects us with who we all are at the center. That is love. We all have 1 thing in common, we have hearts. That's what connects us. Humans, nature, earth, and all livings beings. But these different thoughts and beliefs that we have developed, that are not ours is not only what separates us from ourselves, (love) but also all the love around us. Reconnect. Daily self-love.

Oct 30th Just breathe

I challenge you to belly breathe right now, and 5 times throughout the day. Placing your hands on your belly and experiencing the rise and fall of your belly. With each inhale and exhale. Always taking note of how you feel before and after.

NOVEMBER

Nov 1st Self-love

Write 8 things that you love about yourself. Get creative it can be anything.

Nov 2nd Love is the key

Let love be your only language.

Nov 3rd Reminder

Let your heart be your mediator.

Nov 4th Center

Take ten deep breaths right now as big, slow, and controlled as you can. With every exhale, experience the feeling of weight being removed from your shoulders. Notice how you feel now, as opposed to before you did it. I challenge you to take ten more 10-second interval deep breaths throughout your day.

Nov 5th Love is the key

Make decisions based on love, not fear.

Nov 6th Ask yourself

Are you 100% happy and fulfilled with who you are and where you are in your life at this moment?

Ok, now ask yourself are you always 100% true and authentic in every moment and situation in your life?

Are you making all your decisions out of love or from fear?

Ok, now if you answered yes to #2 and #3 was no. To change #1, you have to change 2 and 3.

Nov 7th

Spend 30 seconds 5 x's alone today just focusing on your inhale and exhale breathing.

Nov 8th Reconnect

Spend at least 10 minutes in nature today. Walking the ground without shoes. Allow mother earth to recharge and reground you.

Nov 9th

If all religions would see what they are doing... Dividing themselves from each other. Thinking what they believe is better than the next. (judgement) Religion is creating what? (separation) Love is not judgment. Love is not separation. Love is unity. Love is the only truth.

Nov 10th

Religion gives people hope. Only you yourself can give you love. (fulfillment) We are all love. So, to love thyself fully (home) is to love all living beings (earth, nature, animals) because they are love. We are one love.

Nov 11th

Everyone has the same desire. To love and be loved. You are what you're seeking love). I'm only telling you to love (thyself). Thyself being love. (home)

Nov 12th Notes to self

Discipline your body. Discipline your mind. (beliefs) If these are sound. Nothing can penetrate your heart. (love)

Nov 13th

You must work from the inside out. The internal battle that you are facing (beliefs, thoughts, emotions) are things you cannot touch, grab, or see. They cannot be resolved with things outside of ourselves. (people, places, things, $$)

Nov 14th

Love.

Love.

Nov 15th Ask yourself

Am I being my most authentic and truest self in every situation and circumstance? If not, you have no one to blame other than yourself for any transgressions and negativity you may be facing in your life.

Nov 16th Ask yourself

Are you following your heart and trusting your intuition in every situation and circumstance? Again, if not, you have no one to blame other than yourself for any transgressions and negativity you may be facing in your life.

Nov 17th Monthly drawing

Think back to your childhood and visualize something from your childhood. Capture that image. Now draw it. No expectations. No worrying about if you're doing it right or how it looks. Just being free and allowing creativity to take over.

Nov 18th Reminder

You are love and you are loved.

Nov 19th Ask yourself

Does your life revolve around money, food, and sex? (survival) Or does it revolve around love? (peace)

Nov 20th

The only job you should be interested in. Is getting to know u. Most people are putting in 8-hour work days for companies that could care less about their mental well-being and heart. If you put that much energy in something you know doesn't love you...Why not put that into yourself?

Nov 21st

Be your own motivation and inspiration, allow the love you have for yourself to drive and motivate you daily. There is nothing wrong with acknowledging and appreciating all the love and inspiration you garner from other people, places, and things. But that outside source of love and inspiration may not always be there.

Nov 22nd

If your cup is filled always you'll never feel like you need something or someone outside of yourself to fill your own cup. It's yours. (self-love)

Nov 23rd

Don't let your mind guide your heart. Instead allow your heart to guide your mind. Let love take the lead.

Nov 24th Letting go of attachment

I challenge you today to spend 4-5 hours with your phone off, or without touching or using your phone. Our phone is just a tool to be used when needed, not relied on heavily or attached to.

Nov 25th

If you don't wake up excited to be you and enjoy the everyday journey of life, reevaluate yourself and your life. Examine what is causing you not to be excited about being you and you getting to be you.

Nov 26th

Find comfort in the solitude of your heart and mind opposed to finding temporary comfort in things outside of yourself. These things can lead to false expectations of comfort.

Nov 27th

Love is meant to harmonize differences. Write down 3 ways you will allow more love into your personal relationships. (self-included) Harmonize and iron out some differences you may have past or present.

____

____

____

____

Nov 28th — Daily to do list

Meditate. Reconnect. Let go. Just be. Create more. Consume less. Live limitlessly.

Nov 29th — Notes to self

I'm not within the confinement of my body. My body is within the confinement of my soul. My soul is infinite and limitless.

Nov 30th

How people allow others to treat them is a very good depiction of how they view themselves. So. KNOW your worth. Value you and who you are.

DECEMBER

Dec 1st Self-love

Write 8 things that you love about yourself. Get creative it can be anything.

Dec 2nd Love is the key

Love should always be the first option.

Dec 3rd

See with love. Speak with love. Hear with love. Think of love. Today when you are doing all 4 of these acts...Ask yourself am I doing this with love?

Dec 4th

You are not here to be perfect. You are not here to live up to some expectations or standards that may have been placed on you from (people, place, and things) your only duty to is to be authentic, just be you.

Dec 5th Reminder

You are loved.

Dec 6th Perspective

Use every situation that may appear to be working against you to open your heart more and cultivate patience.

Dec 7th

Spend 30 seconds 5 x's alone today just focusing on your inhale and exhale breathing.

Dec 8th ` Challenge

Today give out 10 compliments to people you don't know. Give love.

Dec 9th Listen to your heart

Avoid over analyzing the decisions you make. Instead do what feels right in your heart and out of love. Remember the universe supports you in all your decision making. Be confident.

Dec 10th

My open book journal: Written April 3rd, 2017

I get it. That missing puzzle piece. That absent something. We all carry that same feeling. Like something is missing. We can never quite pinpoint it. But we feel it. Like some void or something that is missing from within your life as to why you are just not satisfied. It Has ALWAYS been me. But the way we are taught and all these beliefs that are placed on us unwillingly since birth that aren't yours. All that we are continually consuming from our parents, friends, society, and the media begins to mold us with "beliefs" and thoughts that aren't actually ours. Which leads us to believe that, that missing something, that void that is unfilled, that missing puzzle piece, is something that is outside of ourselves. So, we begin to overcompensate by obtaining more such as relationships, car, money, having kids, jobs, material things and we have these expectations thinking all these externals will fill that void, that it'll be that missing puzzle piece, ultimately being led back to the same realization these things can only provide me with a momentary feeling of fulfillment. But after that momentary feeling that goes away, you're led back to that same initial feeling. Somethings missing. And it becomes a cycle. We begin to obtain more.

Consume more. In hopes, that void will be filled. But the more you consume, the more you obtain, the more you seek guidance and answers outside of yourself. Which is what we have been doing since we began this human experience. Consuming. It clouds our mind; our thoughts add more beliefs that aren't ours and molds us into this character or identity that isn't actually us. And we begin to live through this character of who we "think" we are. Based on all of what we have consumed, been taught, believed, and thought to think are ours. But we did not create them. Something as simple as our name was given to us unwilling. We didn't even have a say in that, but we go through life, living this truth. Thinking this is it. Considering this is who we are. Not even knowing why we are the way we are, and why we do what we do, or feel the way that we do. We go through life unhappy, unfilled, we settle for complacency, we marginalize ourselves. We tell ourselves we aren't capable of this or that. We take all the power we have to create and live freely out of our hands. So, with that said. That missing puzzle piece, that missing void, that little something that you feel is not there. Has been, and always will be you. Reconnect with YOU. Let go of all that you've consumed since you took in that first air of breath. Before you knew you had this name, this job, this and that. You weren't born with any of this. It was given. Reconnect with your childhood essence. Meditate. Clear your mind of all that is not yours. Which is ultimately everything. Because we are all born into this life a blank slate. We literally can be and do whatever we desire. Reclaim your power. You are infinite. You are everything. We are all connected. We are all but a collection of thoughts and experiences, molding each other unconsciously, and consciously. Become aware. Liberate yourself mentally. Follow your heart, trust your intuition, and know your mind can do all things. Mediate. Meditate. Meditate. Clear your mind of all those thoughts and beliefs that have held you captive thus far. Reconnect with your true childlike essence, to your wholeness and oneness. LM.

Much love.

Dec 11th

Embrace compliments. We are quick to absorb the negative things people say about us and then we hold on to them. But it is hard to accept and believe the compliments that are given to us.

Dec 12th

Let everything you do be because you have a desire to do it. Not because you are seeking outside validation.

Dec 13th

No expectations: Pat yourself on the back. Do not expect someone to do it for you. But if someone decides to pat you on the back. Embrace it. Accept it. Love it, but without attachment. Always know that if those pats disappear. The pats you give yourself will never stop, and they are the #1 most important accolade. None can compare. Be free of expectation. Never expect others to always be there. Just enjoy them for their worth.

Dec 14th

Let go of the belief that something outside of yourself will give you true fulfillment.

Dec 15th

If you're not happy with what you do for a living. Why do it? Let go of the fear of change and uncertainty. Do exactly what your heart desires. No more, what if. Only WHAT WILL BE.

Dec 16th

To open your mind is to approach people, places, and things free of opinions.

Dec 17th

Instead of approaching people in your life with a preconceived thought. Always look for yourself in them. Opposed to approaching them with some pre-conceived thought or belief that isn't even yours. Look for yourself in them. To gain a better understanding of them, but more importantly yourself. We serve as mirrors.

Dec 18th

This book has not suggested you worship or believe in anything. Other than yourself. Yourself being love. And we are all love.

Dec 19th

There is only 1 sin in this life and this is to not love. You are love. You were born love. We are all born love. We are all love (thyself) (nature, earth, animals, humans). Don't let these external things (religions, people, places, things) (beliefs) keep you from reconnecting with love. (thyself)

Dec 20th

Monthly drawing

Think back to your childhood and visualize something from your childhood. Capture that image. Now draw it. No expectations. No worrying about if you're doing it right or how it looks. Just be free and allow creativity to take over.

Dec 21st

Things we hear and perceive as hurtful or bad from people don't hurt us because of who said them, or even how they said it. But more so, what they said reminds us of the thoughts we already have about ourselves. Things we try to ignore most times. Overcome these negative thoughts you have about yourself so that hurtful words that come from others will no longer harm you (self-love). "Confidence isn't saying they will like me. Confidence is saying I'll be good, if they don't."

Dec 22nd

Never anticipate negativity when entering a situation new or old. You get what you put in most times. If you are creating negative energy around a situation or circumstance, that's what you'll produce.

Dec 23rd Ask yourself

What would you spend your time doing if money didn't exist at all?

Dec 24th

Written June 28th, 2018, question asked:

"How did you start your journey?"

Just asking myself why?

Why am I this way?

Why do I have low self-confidence?

Why do I have self-doubt?

I knew I was dope, talented, creative and had so much to offer the world and people around me. But my thoughts didn't coincide with that. I knew I wasn't born with any of these thoughts and beliefs. So, I had to dive deep into my mind and thoughts. Through mediation and just thinking I relived all my experiences from childhood until now. Pinpointing all the negative beliefs and thoughts I picked up from those experiences I had been through that molded me into someone I knew I wasn't. I am breaking free of those mental traps. A LOT of hard work. Training my body. Then my mind to lead me back to my heart.

Dec 25th Food for thought

Think about how quick we are to place expectations on others and how mad we get when they don't live up to these expectations. But we ourselves have not lived up to our own personal expectations.

Dec 26th Reevaluate

Get back to the root of how you've developed false identities, unrecognizable character traits, trained negative reactions, perceptions you associate with, and self-hate you've inflicted on yourself. Unroot it and create new loving nuances for yourself.

Dec 27th

Let go of the narrative of who you believe you should be. And just be.

Dec 28th

All more $$ does is bring comfort and stability. But not peace, love, or fulfillment.

Dec 29th

Pain is temporary. Circumstances are temporary. Heartbreak is temporary. Fear makes all these things appear to be permeant. When love is the only the permanent force.

Dec 30th

No longer battle with your mind (ego) and your heart (love). Unify the two, so your ego is advocating what stems from your heart (love) and not what's stemming from your mind. Use beliefs and thoughts that you have accumulated from experiences that you perceived as negative or bad.

Dec 31st

Go back and re-read every 1st day of each month.

Index

www.ingramcontent.com/pod-product-compliance
Lightning Source LLC
Chambersburg PA
CBHW071420090426
42737CB00011B/1524